'*A Christian's Pocket Guide to Islam* constitutes a good introduction to the faith of Muslims. It clearly and concisely describes the major facets of that faith and is punctuated with helpful insights for those seeking positive ways to relate as Christian witnesses to Muslims. The Guide also conveys a heart-concern for those who live precariously as Christians in Muslim-majority cultures.'

**Rev. Dr Bill Musk,
former missionary in the Middle East, author of
three books on Christians relating to Muslims**

'It is a pleasure to commend this little book to Christians who would like to be better equipped to share their faith with Muslim friends. Written for those with no prior knowledge of Islam, this book gives all the basic facts which will help a Christian to be more effective in their witness, as well as helpful guidance on how to approach Muslims lovingly and appropriately.'

**Zafar Ismail, chairman,
Interserve's Ministry Among Asians in Britain
and formerly director of the
Open Theological Seminary, Pakistan**

A Christian's Pocket Guide to

Islam

Patrick Sookhdeo

Isaac Publishing
and
CHRISTIAN FOCUS

Copyright © Patrick Sookhdeo 2001

ISBN 1-84550-119-5

10 9 8 7 6 5 4 3 2 1

First published in 2001,
reprinted in 2001, 2002 (twice), 2003, 2004
This edition published in 2005
by
Christian Focus Publications,
Geanies House, Fearn,
Ross-shire, IV20 1TW Scotland
and
Isaac Publishing,
The Old Rectory, River Street, Pewsey,
Wiltshire, SN9 5DB England
on behalf of
Fellowship of Faith for the Muslims
and the
Institute for the Study of Islam and Christianity

www.christianfocus.com

Cover design by Danie Van Straaten

Printed and bound by
Norhaven Paperback A/S, Viborg

CONTENTS

For the sake of simplicity for English readers, Arabic terms have been transliterated without diacritical marks. For example, 'Quran' rather than 'Qur'an'. Italics are used for words which are not common in English usage.

All quotations from the Quran are taken from the translation by Abdullah Yusuf Ali (Beltsville, Maryland: Amana Publications, 1995).

<u>Important Note:</u> The Quran is divided into chapters called surahs, which are subdivided into verses (ayahs). References are given with the surah number first, followed by the verse number, like a Bible reference. However, Quranic verse numbers vary slightly in different printings of the Quran. To find the quotations in this booklet, it may be necessary to check the verses that precede or follow the references given.

PREFACE

The purpose of this book is to outline the beliefs and practices of the religion of Islam, in order to help Christians to share their faith more effectively with their Muslim friends and neighbours.

It is based on a compilation of a number of booklets previously published by Fellowship of Faith for the Muslims under the series title 'Focus on Islam', and then published in 1997 as 'A Pocket Guide to Islam'. This has now been expanded with additional material.

Although Islam and Christianity have certain points of doctrine in common, there is an enormous difference between them, not only in beliefs about salvation and Christ, but also in many other areas affecting daily life, attitudes and worldviews. It is vital that the Christian who desires to make known the Gospel of our Lord Jesus Christ to Muslims should understand something of the assumptions and convictions which their hearer is likely to hold. This knowledge helps the Christian to avoid creating some unnecessary stumbling blocks and difficulties for their Muslim friend. This book includes some comparisons and contrasts with biblical teaching where this is most relevant for witnessing to Muslims.

Within Islam there are many variations, just as within Christianity. A short book like this must generalize and simplify, so the reader should not be surprised if their Muslim friend takes a different stance on certain minor areas.

The attitude of a Christian seeking to share the Gospel with a Muslim must not be one of antagonism, conflict or hatred. We must approach our Muslim friends peaceably and humbly, with the attitude and mind of Christ, the servant King (Phil. 2:5-8). We must be careful also of our vocabulary concerning witnessing to Muslims. We should avoid words reminiscent of warfare or colonialism. Such terminology does a grave disservice to the Gospel. Our words should be gracious (Col. 4:6).

Our approach should also be characterized by accuracy in everything. We must not misrepresent Islam or accuse Muslims of beliefs and practices which are not theirs. Furthermore, we must remember always that Muslims are people, ordinary human beings like ourselves, with the joys, sorrows, fears and anxieties that we ourselves experience. We must be filled with the compassion of Christ, compelled by His love (2 Cor. 5:14). Yet we must also be completely faithful to Christ. We cannot alter, bend or dilute His teachings in any way.

It is important too that Christians who engage in ministry to Muslims should recognize that Islam is not just a theology but a real spiritual power, one of those powers about which Paul writes in

Ephesians 6.12. Christians will need to be spiritually prepared for this encounter.

It is my prayer that this pocket guide will be used of God to equip Christian believers to bring many Muslims to the joy and assurance of a living relationship with Jesus Christ as Lord and Saviour.

Patrick Sookhdeo

ONE

THE ORIGINS OF ISLAM

Islam is the name given to the religion founded by
Muhammad in Arabia in the early seventh century.
The word *ISLAM* is derived from the verb *SLM* to
resign, surrender, submit oneself, and *iSLaM* means
the act of submission and of resignation of oneself.
One who professes Islam is a *muSLiM*, one who has
submitted. It is said by Muslims to be the religion of
all the prophets from Adam to Muhammad.

Muhammad
(See also Appendix I)

His background

Muhammad was born in the wealthy merchant town of
Mecca, which was a very important trading centre for
western Arabia. It stood on the main caravan routes
joining the land-borne trade of the Arabian peninsula
with the maritime trade of the Red Sea, thus linking
India to the West and Africa to Persia.

Mecca was also famous for its shrine, the Kaba.
This cube-like building was the centre of a cult of
sacred stones including the 'Black Stone', said to
have come from heaven, which is built into the eastern

corner of the Kaba. The Kaba was a centre of annual pilgrimage for tribes throughout Arabia.

The religious situation in Arabia before the advent of Islam is referred to by Muslim historians as 'the times of ignorance'. The Arabs were largely idolatrous and polytheistic as well as mostly animists, worshipping the stars, for example. According to some sources, as many as 360 deities were worshipped at the Kaba.

Jewish and Christian communities had settled in Arabia. The Jews, being traders, had settled in the trading cities on the caravan routes, taking with them their rabbis, Scriptures and synagogues. From the Jews, the Arabs gained a superficial knowledge of the Old Testament stories and Jewish folklore, which is seen in the pages of the Quran.

The Christianity that Muhammad encountered was brought to Arabia chiefly by Christians who had fled from the Byzantine Empire, victims of the intricate Christological controversies of those days, who had been condemned as heretics. Muhammad's very imperfect understanding of Christian doctrine was probably due to the nature of these informants.

His early life
The earliest accounts of Muhammad's life were written at least 150 years after his death. All are Muslim sources, and there is no external (i.e. non-Muslim) supporting evidence.

Muhammad was born in A.D. 570 or 571, a few months after the death of his father Abdullah. His family belonged to the Quraysh tribe, at that time the custodians of the Kaba. His mother Aminah died when he was six. He was brought up by his paternal uncle, Abu Talib. Tradition says that, on a caravan convoy with his uncle, he met a Nestorian monk who, according to some Muslim commentators, perceived that Muhammad was a prophet. When Muhammad grew up to manhood, he became an esteemed member of the merchants' guild at Mecca. He joined the caravan trading routes, making contacts with Jews and Christians, with whom he discussed religion in connection with the Old and New Testaments.

Many non-Muslims have thought Muhammad to be a deliberate imposter, but perhaps he was at first a genuine seeker after divine truth, who was dissatisfied with the Christian witness of his time as well as the idolatrous state of his own people in Arabia.

Muhammad was employed by Khadijah, a wealthy widow, to manage her caravan trade. Although she was fifteen years his senior, Muhammad married Khadijah when he was twenty-five. The marriage produced seven children (three boys and four daughters), all of whom died young, except a daughter, Fatimah, who became the wife of Ali-ibn-Abu Talib and mother of Hassan and Hussain. Khadijah died twenty-five years later. After her death Muhammad married a further twelve wives, thereby sanctioning polygamy.

His later life and call
By his marriage Muhammad became a person of importance and was able to find time for uninterrupted meditation on religious matters. At about the age of

forty, he became very concerned about the irreligion of his fellow countrymen and began to retire frequently for meditation to a cave on the slopes of Mount Hirah, some three miles from Mecca. During these periods of meditation, he seemed at times to be in a kind of trance; whilst in this condition he claimed he heard the voice of Allah or of the Archangel Gabriel, who gave him messages to preach to mankind.

The first converts
Muhammad's first followers were chiefly members of his own family – his wife Khadijah, his nephew Ali-ibn-Abu Talib and Zaid, an adopted son who had formerly been his slave, a gift to Muhammad from Khadijah. The first adult outside the family to make profession of Islam was Abu Bakr, a wealthy merchant, who was a significant early convert.

Muhammad's flight to Medina
and the development of his teaching
Most of the inhabitants of Mecca rejected Muhammad's teaching about the true Allah and his warning of the coming judgment. They accused him of being a soothsayer or demon-possessed. Growing hostility on the part of the rulers and people of the city led to violent persecution of the Muslims. Nevertheless there was a gradual increase in his followers, who numbered approximately fifty during the period 610–613.

As the opposition intensified, Muhammad decided to leave Mecca and seek asylum elsewhere. He first sent a number of his followers to the Christian kingdom of Abyssinia, but he himself settled at Yathrib, a city 250 miles north of Mecca, which is now called Medina [city, i.e. the Prophet's own city]. The people of Medina were favourably disposed towards Muhammad and the new teaching. He had been invited there by a party of its inhabitants who had met him, accepted his claims and prepared their fellow townsmen for his advent. The citizens, wearied by long internal strife, were ready to welcome a strong leader who might unite them. Jews and Christians were at this time sympathetic to Muhammad's teaching with its emphasis on the unity of God and accompanying condemnation of idolatry.

The move from Mecca to Medina took place in the year 622. This flight or hijrah was the turning point in Muhammad's career, and was chosen to mark the beginning of the Muslim era and calendar. In 624 Muhammad's forces gained a decisive victory at the Battle of Badr. The decision to give shares in the booty to those who fought with him swung the military balance in his favour. Henceforth, war on religious grounds was sanctioned and the jihad [holy war] became not only acceptable but a religious duty for Muslims when Islam is under threat.

At first Muhammad recognized the validity of the Jewish and Christian faiths, being content to preach as the prophet to his own people. Jerusalem was chosen as the direction which a Muslim should face when praying, and he adopted several Jewish practices. However friction developed when the Jewish tribes failed to recognize him as a true prophet or to practise the customs of Islam. Troubled by this, Muhammad began to assert the absolute character of the revelation that had been given to him, and claimed that it was a renewal of the religion that Abraham had professed. In this way he gave up any attempt to reconcile Islam with Judaism. The Muslim community were now commanded to face the Kaba at Mecca when praying, not Jerusalem as previously.

During Muhammad's time in Medina, his doctrine took shape. Not only the direction of prayer, but also other areas of his early teaching were modified. At Medina, he began to teach that the Quran was the final and superior revelation. The daily times of prayer with preliminary washings now became obligatory. Friday was appointed the day for corporate worship at the mosque. The annual month of fasting was established.

In Medina Muhammad became statesman, legislator and judge. As his power and influence increased so did large-scale warfare. In the eight years following the hijrah, Muslim armies succeeded in conquering the whole of Arabia and stamping on it the religion of Islam. Muhammad was the first person to unify the Arabs as one people.

The death of Muhammad and the expansion of Islam
(See Appendix II)

Muhammad died in 632 at the age of sixty-two and was succeeded as Caliph by Abu Bakr, one of his earliest followers. Under Abu Bakr, Islam was consolidated as a stable power, and Syria fell to its advancing armies.

Abu Bakr was succeeded in 634 by Caliph Umar, who was in turn succeeded by Caliph Uthman in 644. During this time Iraq, Persia and Egypt fell in quick succession, and by 656 the boundaries of Islam had reached Afghanistan in the east, Libya in the west and the Caucasus mountains in the north. The conquest of the remainder of North Africa and advance through Spain into France was only halted in 732 at one of history's crucial battles, fought on a site between Tours and Poitiers.

Reasons for such a rapid expansion are not hard to find. The collapse of the Byzantine Empire had created a political vacuum. This the dynamic leadership of Muhammad was able to exploit. The Arab peoples, for so long divided along tribal lines, were united under their new leadership and more able to make a positive thrust, first into the lands surrounding the Arabian peninsula and then further afield into North Africa and Europe.

With the notable exception of the Copts in Egypt, the Christian Church in North Africa was defeated and overthrown. The Church which had known the leadership of such men as Augustine, Athanasius, Cyprian and Tertullian found itself quite unable to resist the advancing armies of Islam. The ruins of ancient church buildings are the sole remains of a once vigorous Church.

Two

Islamic Teaching

Faith and works

The religion of Islam demands of its believers firstly *iman* [faith], which their theologians define as 'confession with the tongue and belief with the heart'. This confession runs: 'I perceive (and bear witness) that there is no god except Allah and I perceive (and bear witness) that Muhammad is the Messenger of God.' This statement is known as the *shahada* or *kalima*.

The second requirement is for *din* [religion], in the sense of 'works' or practical duties, of which there are five in number. Because of their fundamental importance these obligations are known as *arkan-ud-din* [the pillars of religion].

The six articles of faith

The six articles of faith in which Muslims must believe are:

1. God [Allah]
The unity of Allah is clearly taught in the Quran. Like the Bible, the Quran does not argue for the existence of God. It assumes that Allah is. The oneness of Allah

is the first article of the *kalima*: 'There is no deity but Allah [*la ilah ill Allahu*].' This positive assertion is found frequently in the Quran. Similarly there is the repeated affirmation that *shirk*, the 'giving of partners to Allah' is the worst of sins. Allah is one, having no equal and no partner. Omnipotence and omniscience are ascribed to Allah and are thought to safeguard both his unity and his majesty.

2. Angels [malaikah]

Angels are frequently mentioned in the Quran. They are created beings, made of light, and are referred to as 'messengers of Allah' with specific functions. They watch over humans and some record their deeds, both good and bad. They also surround the throne of Allah to sing his praise. The greatest is Jibrail [Gabriel], the revealer of Allah to Muhammad, who is also called *Rul ul'Amin*, the Holy Spirit. It is he who strengthened Jesus. The other archangels include Mikail [Michael] the provider, Israfil the trumpeter of doom, and Izrail the custodian who has the care of the faithful at death.

Contrasted with the angels are the jinn, some good, some evil. They were created by Allah out of smokeless fire before he created Adam out of clay (Q 15:26). These shadowy spirits frequent ruined houses, desert places, and certain mountains and wells. Many Muslims live in dread of evil jinn and take various precautions to protect themselves from attack.

The devil, whose name is Iblis or Shaytan [Satan], is sometimes described as a jinn and sometimes as an angel.

3. Books [kutub]

Muslims believe that Allah has revealed his commands to men through his prophets and through 104 sacred books. Of these books, only four now remain, believed to have been given to Moses (the *Taurah* i.e. the Pentateuch), David (the *Zabur*, the Psalms), Jesus (the *Injil*, the Gospels or the New Testament in general) and Muhammad (the Quran). It is claimed that Jews and Christians, described jointly as *ahl-al-kitab* [the people of the book], changed and distorted their own Scriptures, so Allah sent the Quran as the final revelation to mankind.

4. Prophets [nabi]

Through prophets Allah has mercifully deigned to intervene in human history, in order to remind humans of the last day and the life hereafter and to guide them in all the activities of life on the right path which leads towards final election. The same truths were revealed by the earlier prophets before Muhammad's arrival. He links up with the faith of Abraham and ends the ever-recurring gaps between the prophets. As the final messenger, he is often referred to as 'the seal of the prophets'.

A Muslim cannot deny any of the prophets of the Old Testament or John the Baptist and Jesus in the New Testament (Q 2:285). Of the many prophets, only nine are regarded as major prophets. These are Noah, Abraham, David, Jacob, Joseph, Job, Moses, Jesus and Muhammad. Muhammad is the only prophet mentioned in the Quran who is not mentioned in the

Old or New Testaments, though Muslims think that
some of the references to the coming Holy Spirit
were prophecies about Muhammad. The list of Islamic prophets also includes many characters not
occurring in the Bible, in fact not known anywhere
else at all.

Muslims do not worship Muhammad or any of the
prophets but consider them examples and models for
mankind. They dislike being called 'Muhammadans'
because they are not worshippers of Muhammad,
but of Allah. None of the prophets are considered
divine.

*5. Day of judgment [yawm al-akhirah] and resurrec-
tion after death [basi bad al-maut]*
The day of judgment is described vividly in the Quran
and is closely connected with the resurrection. The
day will be preceded by clear signs and natural ca-
tastrophes, the appearance of the Antichrist [*Dajjal*],
tumults and seditions, commotion in heaven and earth
(Q 101:1-5; 70:9-10), the darkening of the sun and
moon (Q 75:8; 81:1) and Christ's second coming, as
a Muslim (see pages 21-2, 40). On the last day:

> The trumpet will (just)
> Be sounded, when all
> That are in the heavens
> And on earth will swoon,
> Except such as it will
> Please Allah (to exempt).
> Then will a second one

    Be sounded, when, behold,
    They will be standing
    And looking on! (Q 39:68)

After the resurrection people will wander about for
forty years, during which time the books containing
the records of their deeds kept by the recording angels
will be given up. Then will follow the weighing of the
deeds on the eschatological scales [mizan].

    Then those whose balance
    (Of good deeds) is heavy –
    They will attain salvation.
    But those whose balance
    Is light, will be those
    Who have lost their souls;
    In Hell will they abide. (Q 23:102, 103)

Then everybody, believers and unbelievers, has to
cross a very narrow bridge [sirat]. Some Muslims will
be saved immediately, some will fall off the bridge into
hell and afterwards be released. The infidels will all
fall into hell and remain there for ever.

6. Allah's sovereign decrees – predestination [taqdir]
Muslim devotion attributes to Allah supreme and
sovereign power over all things. The Muslim believer
must submit to Allah's will. The doctrine of absolute
predestination is widespread (see page 46). Maktub
[it is written], maqdur [it is decided] and kismat [it
is my lot] are expressions commonly used to express
this fatalism.

Shariah – Islamic Law

Islamic teaching is derived not only from the Quran but also from the hadith, that is, collections of traditions recording the words and deeds of Muhammad. These traditions are accorded an importance second only to the Quran, and provide the Muslim faithful with many of the detailed instructions for their religious practice and daily life, based on the pattern of Muhammad's own life.

Where the Quran and traditions are silent on a particular subject, rules are derived by consensus of the religious leaders [*ijma*] and by analogous reasoning [*qiyas*]. The combination of Quran, hadith, *ijma* and *qiyas* have been used by Islamic scholars to create the immensely detailed body of rules and regulations known as the Shariah, that is, Islamic law.

Four orthodox schools are recognized in Sunni Islam:

Hanafi: founded by Imam abu Hanifa (died 767)
Maliki: founded by Imam Malik ibn Anas (died 795)
Shafii: founded by Imam Muhammad bin Idris ash Shafi'i (died 820)
Hanbali: founded by Imam Ahmad ibn Hanbal (died 855)

The Shiah version of Islamic law is very similar and does not differ more from the Sunni schools than they do from each other.

One of the most important differences between Islam and Christianity is the existence of this detailed body of religious law. It regulates not only every aspect of a Muslim's devotional and personal life, but also the governing of an Islamic state. Compiled at a time when Islam was very much in the ascendant politically and militarily, the Shariah makes the assumption that political power lies in the hands of the conquering Muslims. There are many rules relating to non-Muslims, mainly Jews and Christians, who are called *dhimmi* and treated as a conquered and subjugated people. *Dhimmi* are considered second-class citizens and must adhere to a number of restrictions designed to reinforce this second-class status. They have to pay a special tax called *jizya*.

Another feature of the Shariah are the draconian punishments for certain crimes, such as amputation for theft, stoning for adultery etc. Of particular relevance to the Christian evangelist is the death sentence for any Muslim who leaves the faith, which is considered equivalent to treason against the state. While the details of how to apply this rule vary between the different schools of law, all are agreed that an adult male Muslim apostate must be killed.

The attitude of the Shariah to women is very medieval. Like non-Muslims, they are considered of less value than Muslim men, and this is reflected in many rules concerning inheritance, compensation, legal testimony etc. They are restricted by numerous rules ensuring their modesty and preventing them from leading men astray. This stance conflicts with liberal western culture.

It is often argued that the Shariah was quite moderate and lenient by contemporary standards at the time of its creation in the eighth and ninth centuries. It has remained unchanged since then, and is extremely harsh by modern western standards, infringing many areas of human rights, including the right to choose one's faith.

The strict sanctions against any who deviate from the existing rules has ensured that the Shariah has survived unchanged for eleven centuries. The question of whether and how much it can be changed and adapted for the modern world is one which is debated within Islam today. The rise of radical Islam, which began in the middle of the twentieth century and continues now in the twenty-first, has made this debate a dangerous one for moderates who advocate change and liberalization. They are liable to be condemned as heretics or apostates and assassinated.

No country of the world today rules according to the full Shariah. However, many contain elements of it within their legislation. For example, the rule that apostates from Islam should be executed is part of the state law in Saudi Arabia, Iran and Sudan, to name but three.

Even where Shariah is not legally enforced, the attitudes behind it are very prevalent amongst the Muslim community. Christian minorities in Muslim-majority contexts are commonly despised and discriminated against by society at large. They may find it hard to gain examination passes, get a job, get promotion or get justice from the police and judiciary. They are thought of and treated as *dhimmi*, even if the constitution and laws guarantee equality of all citizens. Similarly, the position of women shows the influence of Shariah on culture, even without legal enforcement. The Shariah's teaching that apostasy from Islam is like treason results in terrible shame being felt by a Muslim family if one of their members converts to Christianity. There will normally be rejection of the convert and sometimes violence, even murder, in accordance with the Shariah's death penalty for an apostate. While this extreme is more common in Muslim countries where the law-enforcement officers are likely to sympathize with the murderer's motives, it has happened even in the West in modern times.

The ultimate goal of Muslim radicals is to introduce full Shariah as widely as possible in the world, and thus create an Islamic state similar to that in Medina in Muhammad's time.

Jesus in Islam

Jesus has a prominent place in the Quran. He is referred to as 'Son of Mary' or 'Jesus, son of Mary', and four times as 'the Messiah [Christ], son of Mary'. Though regarded as a prophet sent from Allah, His deity and atoning death are strenuously denied. Some interpreters of the Quran maintain that He did not die, but rather that Allah frustrated the plans of the Jews by allowing another man to be crucified in his place. Muslims believe that Jesus will come back to earth as a Muslim, will marry and have children, then die and be buried near Muhammad. Some traditions assert that at this second coming He will destroy every cross, kill all Jews, convert the Christians to Islam, and reign as king of all Muslims.

(See also the Quran's affirmations and denials about Christ, pages 33-40.)

The Muslim calendar

This calendar was adopted by Muslims in about A.D. 632. The starting point (year 1) is the hijrah, which occurred on 16 July 622 according to the Christian calendar. Years are designated 'A.H.' for 'after hijrah'.

The years are purely lunar and consist of twelve months containing in alternate sequence 30 or 29 days, with occasional adjustments of an additional day at the end of the twelfth month. The year is thus only 354 days long. The ninth month in each Muslim year (Ramadan) is observed as a fast. The pilgrimage to Mecca must be made in the twelfth month. The names of the Islamic months are as follows:

Muharram
Safar
Rabi al-awwal
Rabi al-thani
Jumada al-ula
Jumada al-akhirah
Rajab
Shaban

Ramadan
Shawal
Dhul qadah
Dhul hijjah

Because of its short length, the Muslim year starts about eleven days earlier each time. The regular annual festivals therefore occur on a different date each year when marked on the Christian calendar.

THREE

THE QURAN

Introduction

The Quran, the sacred book of the Muslims, is believed by them to have been revealed to Muhammad by the angel Gabriel 'piecemeal' as occasion required during the last twenty-three years of his life. Muslims take a fundamentalist attitude to God's word, and the Quran holds a place of exalted reverence in their hearts. The Quran is said to have existed eternally in heaven engraved on a stone tablet. The language of this archetype is Arabic. Therefore that language is inherently of a stature unattainable by any other. Speakers of Arabic have a special prestige in the eyes of the Muslim world.

The revelations were passed on orally by Muhammad to his companions, some of whom wrote them down while others memorized them. Muslim orthodoxy holds that the angel Gabriel helped Muhammad to collate the revelations periodically so that at his death there was an exact transcript of what was written on the heavenly tablet.

Modern scholarship, however, has shown that there was no complete set of collated and arranged revelations at Muhammad's death. Some time after his death the revelations were assembled by Muslim leaders from records written on leaves, stones, camel's shoulder-blades etc. and from the memories of those who had stored the revelations in their minds. The resulting collections of revelations made in different places varied somewhat from each other. Caliph Uthman decided to bring order to the situation and had scholars create an official standard text between 650 and 656, which he circulated widely while ordering all other versions to be destroyed.

The oldest surviving fragments of Quranic manuscripts date from no earlier than the second century A.H. (approximately the eighth century A.D.). They are written in a Kufic script showing consonants only. The result is as ambiguous and open to interpretation as if all the vowels and punctuation marks were to be removed from an English text. Vowel points and other helpful marks were added later. Variants continued to exist until at least the tenth century A.D. when some Islamic scholars were imprisoned for refusing to abandon their preferred versions. Even in the mid-twentieth century two versions were still in use, a fact that would be disbelieved by most Muslims. While the majority of the Muslim world had one version, an alternative was still in use in North Africa, though rapidly being ousted by the main version. The Muslim argument that Christians have changed their Scriptures while Muslims have not is therefore clearly inaccurate according to the evidence.

The Quran is about the same length as the New Testament, and is divided into 114 surahs (chapters). The surahs are not arranged in chronological order but roughly in order of length. With the exception of surah 1, which is a prayer addressed to Allah, it is Allah himself and not the prophet who is the speaker.

The word 'Quran' is derived from the Arabic word *qara* meaning 'to read' or 'to recite'. Its use in connection with the Muslim Scriptures is based on the first word of surah 96, which begins: 'Proclaim! (or read!) in the name of thy Lord and Cherisher ....' The first five verses of this surah are generally regarded as the earliest revelation.

The first surah is used daily by Muslims as a prayer, and has a similar place in Islam to the Lord's Prayer in the life of a Christian. It runs:

Praise be to Allah
The Cherisher and Sustainer of the Worlds;
Most Gracious, Most Merciful;
Master of the Day of Judgment.
Thee do we worship,
And Thine aid we seek.
Show us the straight way,
The way of those on whom
Thou hast bestowed Thy Grace,
Those whose (portion)
Is not wrath,
And who go not astray.

The earliest surahs bear some comparison to the psalms in length, subject matter and rhythmic form. They differ in approach, however, as they are not the striving of the human heart after Allah, but Allah speaking to mankind and using the prophet as a mouthpiece. Much else in the Quran deals with matters of legislation for the Muslim community, as well as stories of the prophets.

For the Muslim, the Quran is the word of Allah in the most literal sense. Muhammad was merely the recipient of that word who passed it on. It bears no imprint of the prophet's character at all, and Muslims consider it blasphemous to attribute the Quran even in a secondary sense to Muhammad, as, for example, the writings of the Bible are attributed to their human authors.

The Quran plays a special part in the lives of most Muslims, who have to recite a section or verses from it five times every day in their prayers, and try to learn by heart as many verses as possible. No pious Muslim would ever drink, smoke, or make a noise while the Quran is being read aloud. The chanting of the Quran in Arabic has a pleasing – even hypnotic – effect on the Arabic-speaking person; this cannot be conveyed in an English translation.

Although it does not deal with all aspects of life for which Islam legislates, in those areas in which the Quran speaks it does so with absolute divine authority, being the primary source of authority for Muslims. Where there is a contradiction between different parts of the Quran a simple rule is applied to determine

which text to obey: the later verse annuls the earlier
one. The term 'abrogation' is generally used for this
annulment. The rationale is that the earlier verse
was appropriate to the early stages of Muhammad's
mission, but later different conditions necessitated a
modification. The difficulty, of course, lies in deter-
mining which was in fact the earlier verse.

The testimony of the Quran to itself

It will be noted from the following selections, repre-
sentative of many other verses in the Quran, that the
Quran repeatedly asserts that it is a revelation direct
from Allah. The following verses were 'revealed' to
Muhammad in reply to objections that it was he who
had produced it:

> Say: 'If the whole
> Of mankind and Jinns
> Were to gather together
> To produce the like
> Of this Quran they
> Could not produce
> The like thereof, even if
> They backed up each other
> With help and support.' (Q 17:88)

> This Quran is not such
> As can be produced
> By other than Allah;
> On the contrary it is
> A confirmation of (revelations)
> That went before it,

And a fuller explanation
Of the Book - wherein
There no doubt –
From the Lord of the Worlds.
Or do they say, 'He forged it'?
Say: 'Bring then
A Surah like unto it,
And call (to your aid)
Anyone you can,
Besides Allah, if it be
Ye speak the truth!' (Q 10:37, 38)

The reference to the fact of the Quran verifying what came before it (Q 10:37) is another frequently asserted claim for the Quran, i.e. that it confirms and carries on the revelation previously 'sent down' in the *Taurah* and in the *Injil*. Typical of such claims is the following verse:

It is He [Allah] Who sent down
To thee (step by step),
In truth, the Book,
Confirming what went before it;
And He sent down the Law
(Of Moses) and the Gospel (Of Jesus)
Before this, as a guide to mankind. (Q 3:3)

In reply to the contention of some of Muhammad's opponents that there were obvious contradictions in the Quran, a verse was revealed to settle the matter:

Allah doth blot out
Or confirm what He pleaseth:
With Him is
The Mother of the Book. (Q 13:39)

This is the famous 'verse of abrogation', justifying the practice of letting the later-dated verse annul the earlier. The 'Mother of the Book', i.e. the source of revelation, refers to the eternal original kept in heaven.

One further claim of the Quran for itself should be noticed, namely, that it was revealed in Arabic, the language of the people to whom it was sent down, and not in a foreign language, like the *Taurah* of the Jews and the *Injil* of the Christians:

Alif Lam Ra. These are
The Symbols (or Verses)
Of the Perspicuous Book.
We have sent it down
As an Arabic Quran,
In order that ye may
Learn wisdom. (Q 12:1, 2)

The testimony of the Quran to previous holy books
There are over 120 references in the Quran to the Scriptures of the Jews and the Christians, testifying to their being genuine revelations from Allah. The Jews and Christians were generally known as 'the people of the Book'.

It is important that Christians relating to Muslims should know that Muhammad did not claim to bring a completely new revelation, or to establish a new religion. His concern was to bring his people back to the original religion professed and preached by all the prophets from Adam onwards. The following verse is an illustration of this attitude:

> Say ye: 'We believe
> In Allah, and the revelation
> Given to us, and to Abraham,
> Ismail, Isaac, Jacob,
> And the Tribes, and that given
> To Moses and Jesus, and that given
> To (all) Prophets from their Lord:
> We make no difference
> Between one and another of them:
> And we bow to Allah (in Islam).' (Q 2:136)

Typical of verses which indicate the acceptance by Muhammad of the existing holy books is that found in Q 4:163:

> We have sent thee
> Inspiration, as We sent it
> To Noah and the Messengers
> After him: We sent
> Inspiration to Abraham,
> Ismail, Isaac, Jacob
> And the Tribes, to Jesus,
> Job, Jonah, Aaron and Solomon,
> And to David We gave
> The Psalms.

Muhammad's dependence on the holy books is even
more clearly indicated in Q 10:94 which recommends
consulting the Jews and Christians 'who have been
reading the book from before thee':

> If thou wert in doubt
> As to what We have revealed
> Unto thee, then ask those
> Who have been reading
> The Book from before thee.

The Christian is, therefore, in a very strong position
in inviting the Muslim to read the Scriptures, for the
Quran clearly testifies to their authenticity, and even
advises the perplexed Muslim to consult the Christians about matters of religion which he or she does
not understand. At this point, however, a barrier arises
between the Muslim and the Christian. Any Muslim
who did in fact consult a Christian, or read the Christian Scriptures, would find obvious contradictions to
the teaching of the Quran.

This is a serious problem to the Muslim, for if
the Quran and the other books – the *Taurah, Zabur*
and the *Injil* – are all from Allah, and if the Quran
is a confirmation of the message of the earlier books,
then there should be harmony and continuity, not
contradiction. The only honest conclusion which can
be arrived at from the existence of contradictions is
that either the previous Scriptures are not in fact
revelations from Allah, or the Quran is not in fact a
revelation from Allah. But that is quite contrary to

the plain teaching of the Quran. To escape from this dilemma Muslims have introduced the theory of the corruption of the existing copies of the Scriptures of the Jews and Christians. On this theory, the references in the Quran to the previous Scriptures are to the original books, and not to the present 'corrupt' copies. In support of this theory, the following verse from the Quran is sometimes quoted:

> There is among them
> A section who distort
> The Book with their tongues:
> (As they read) you would think
> It is a part of the Book,
> But it is no part
> Of the Book; and they say,
> 'That is from Allah',
> But it is not from Allah:
> It is they who tell
> A lie against Allah,
> And (well) they know it! (Q 3:78)

One illustration of how this alleged corruption occurred, is the Muslim contention that the reference in John 16:7 (and other places) to the coming of the Holy Spirit as Counsellor was originally a prophecy concerning the coming of Muhammad, another form of whose name is 'Ahmad'. The verse in the Quran to which Muslims commonly refer in this context reads:

> And remember, Jesus,
> The son of Mary, said:

'O Children of Israel!
I am the messenger of Allah
(Sent) to you, confirming
The Law (which came)
Before me, and giving
Glad Tidings of a Messenger
To come after me,
Whose name shall be Ahmad. (Q 61:6)

The Muslim contention is that the Greek word *Para-cletos* (translated 'Counsellor', 'Comforter' or similarly in the Gospel) is a corruption of the original word *Periclutos*, the meaning of which in Arabic is stated to be 'Ahmad'. For further reading, see John Gilchrist's *Is Muhammad foretold in the Bible?*

This, and all other alleged corruptions of the Scriptures, can easily be shown to be without foundation, from the simple fact that complete manuscripts of the Greek New Testament, which go back two centuries or more before the time of Muhammad, are in existence today. These substantiate the text of our present-day versions, and not the Quranic variant.

The affirmations of the Quran about Christ

When witnessing to Muslims, the affirmations of the Quran are in some respects as important as its denials, though less well known. These positive statements fix the picture of Jesus firmly in the Muslim mind. The following are some of the most important affirmations of the Quran.

1. The virgin birth

Some of the longest chapters in the Quran are concerned with Jesus and Mary and the annunciation of the birth of Christ. The following are some extracts:

> Behold! The angels said:
> 'O Mary! Allah giveth thee
> Glad tidings of a Word
> From Him, his name
> Will be Christ Jesus.
> The son of Mary, held in honour
> In this world and the Hereafter
> And of (the company of) those
> Nearest to Allah.' (Q 3:45)
> She said: 'O my Lord!
> How shall I have a son
> When no man hath touched me?'
> He said: 'Even so:
> Allah createth
> What He willeth:
> When He hath decreed
> A Plan, He but saith
> To it, "Be," and it is' (Q 3:47)

Other key passages on Mary are found in Q 19:16, 17, 19-22 and Q 66:12.

2. The assertion that Jesus is a created being

> The similitude of Jesus
> Before Allah is as that of Adam;

He created him from dust,
Then said to him: 'Be'
And he was. (Q 3:59)

Although the obvious intention of this verse is to
establish the fact of Jesus being merely a man, there
could be some ambiguity as to whether the phrase
'He created him' refers to Adam or to Jesus. If the
reference is to Adam, there is, of course, no contradiction of the Christian Scriptures here. It is generally
regarded by Muslims, however, as referring to Jesus.
In any case, this is a verse to which the Christian's
best reply is to state that the Christian Scriptures
also compare Jesus with Adam, not because He is a
created being like Adam, but that, like Adam, He is
the head of a new creation.

3. The miracles
There is a good deal in the Quran (and still more in
other Muslim writings) of the miracles Jesus performed by way of authenticating His mission, but they
are always stated to be 'by the permission of Allah'.
There is no recognition of the fact that Christ had any
inherent divine power. The following verse is a sample
of these statements:

Then will Allah say:
'O Jesus the son of Mary!
Recount My favour
To thee and to thy mother.
Behold! I strengthened thee

With the holy spirit,
So that thou didst speak
To the people in childhood
And in maturity.
Behold! I taught thee
The Book and Wisdom,
The Law and the Gospel.
And behold! thou makest
Out of clay, as it were,
The figure of a bird,
By My leave,
And thou breathest into it,
And it becometh a bird
By My leave,
And thou healest those
Born blind, and the lepers,
By My leave.
And behold! thou
Bringest forth the dead
By My leave.' (Q 5:110)

The denials of the Quran about Christ

The denials of the Quran relate to the basic doctrines concerning Christ. These carry great weight with a Muslim, who believes that they are the Word of Allah expressed in Allah's own words.

1. Denial of the Trinity and of the deity of Christ

Christ Jesus the son of Mary
Was (no more than)
A Messenger of Allah,

And His Word,
Which He bestowed on Mary,
And a Spirit proceeding
From Him: so believe
In Allah and His Messengers.
Say not 'Trinity': desist:
It will be better for you:
For Allah is One God:
Glory be to Him:
(Far exalted is He) above
Having a son. (Q 4:171)

And behold! Allah will say:
'O Jesus the son of Mary!
Didst thou say unto men,
"Worship me and my mother
As gods in derogation of Allah"?
He will say: "Glory to Thee!
Never could I say
What I had no right
(To say)."' (Q 5:116)

It is well to note here that what the Muslim rejects as
the false teaching of some Christian sects, the Christian also rejects. For what Muhammad rejects here
is not the true teaching of Christianity, but what he
thought was its teaching. He understood the Christians
to believe that the Trinity consisted of Father, Mother
(Mary) and Son. No doubt it was the extreme venera-
tion accorded to Mary by Christians whom Muhammad
met which gave rise to this view.

2. Denial of the Sonship of Christ

There are many verses in the Quran which stress the absolute unity of Allah, and by implication deny the Sonship of Christ, and there are others which deny the possibility of Sonship in general, such as the last surah of all which runs in its entirety:

> Say: He is Allah,
> The One and Only;
> Allah, the Eternal, Absolute;
> He begetteth not
> Nor is He begotten;
> And there is none
> Like unto Him. (Q 112)

There are also a number of verses where the Sonship of Christ is specifically denied, such as Q 4:171 already quoted in connection with the Trinity, and the following verses:

> Such (was) Jesus the son
> Of Mary: (it is) a statement
> Of truth, about which
> They (vainly) dispute.
> It is not befitting
> To (the majesty of) Allah
> That He should beget
> A son. (Q 19:34, 35)

Another relevant passage is Q 6:101-6.

The seriousness of the Muslim view of the Christian doctrines of the Trinity and of the deity of Christ, is seen in the following verse:

> Allah forgiveth not
> That partners should be set up
> With Him; but He forgiveth
> Anything else, to whom
> He pleaseth: to set up
> Partners with Allah
> Is to devise a sin
> Most heinous indeed. (Q 4:48)

This is the unpardonable sin of *shirk*. Although *shirk* – associating anyone with Allah as a co-deity – is the most deadly of all sins, what makes the Christian doctrine even more blasphemous in the eyes of the Muslim is the description of Christ as the Son of God. This arises from the fact that the Muslim – or more properly Muhammad – could only think of sonship in terms of a sexual relationship between father and mother. It is probably true to say that the Muslim is less offended by our ascribing deity to Christ, than by our designation of him as the Son of God.

3. Denial of the crucifixion of Christ

This is probably the best known and most basic of all Muslim denials, not least because it is so categorical:

> That they rejected Faith;
> That they uttered against Mary

A grave false charge;
That they said (in boast),
'We killed Christ Jesus
The son of Mary,
The Messenger of Allah'; –
But they killed him not,
Nor crucified him,
But so it was made
To appear to them, . . .

For of a surety
They killed him not –
Nay, Allah raised him up
Unto Himself; and Allah
Is exalted in Power, Wise. (Q 4:156-158)

No Muslim can side-step the categorical denial of the death of Christ contained in this passage, in spite of the fact that it poses a serious difficulty for the thoughtful Muslim. If Christ did not die, that would obviously make Him far superior to other prophets, such as Muhammad, who did die. But to believe He actually did die means denying the Word of Allah, or at least believing that it has been misinterpreted. To escape from this dilemma, Muslim traditions speak of the future return of Christ to this world, his embracing of Islam, and his subsequent death. This position is based on an interpretation of verses like the following:

'So Peace is on me
The day I was born,

The day that I die,
And the day that I
Shall be raised up
To life (again)'!
Such (was) Jesus the son
of Mary. (Q 19:33-4)

To make this verse fit the theory, the most natural
thing would be to alter the order of the words, so
that the phrase 'the day that I die' follows the phrase
'the day that I shall be raised up to life', but such an
alteration would be a sin to the Muslim as it involves
an alteration to the revealed Word of Allah. It is, in
any case, a weak argument, as the very same words
are used in verse 15 of the same surah, in connection
with John the son of Zechariah (John the Baptist),
and no-one would think of altering the order of the
words in this case.

The teaching of the Quran

The following are some of the other subjects which
the Quran speaks about:

1. The Fall

We said, 'O Adam! dwell thou
And thy wife in the Garden;
And eat of the bountiful things therein
As (where and when) ye will; but approach not
this tree
Or ye run into harm and transgression.'

> Then did Satan make them slip
> From the (Garden) and get them out
> Of the state (of felicity) in which
> They had been. We said:
> 'Get ye down, all (ye people),
> With enmity between yourselves...' (Q 2:35-6)

See also Q 7:19ff. and 20:115-123. In this connection it should be noted that the Quran knows nothing of any earthly paradise in Eden. Paradise is in heaven, and it was from heaven to earth that Adam and Eve literally fell.

2. The Devil
The origin and works of Iblis, the devil, are described in Q 7:11-18, which begins as follows:

> It is We who created you
> And gave you shape;
> Then We bade the angels
> Bow down to Adam, and they
> Bowed down; not so Iblis
> He refused to be of those
> Who bow down.

> (Allah) said: 'What prevented
> Thee from bowing down
> When I commanded thee?'
> He said: 'I am better
> Than he: Thou didst create
> Me from fire, and him from clay.'

(Allah) said: 'Get thee down
From this: it is not
For thee to be arrogant
Here: get out, for thou
Art of the meanest (of creatures).'

3. Hell

Hell is a place of fiery torment for sinners:

And what will explain
To thee what Hell-Fire is?
Naught doth it permit
To endure, and naught
Doth it leave alone! –
Darkening and changing
The colour of man! (Q 74:27-9)

Other passages describing hell and those who will go
there include Q 50:24-6 and 78:21-30.

4. Heaven or paradise

The name most frequently given to paradise, the abode
of the blessed, is *janna* [garden]. The description of
paradise in the Quran shows that it is essentially a
place of sensual delights in which there are beautiful
women, couches covered with rich brocades, flowing
cups and luscious fruits.

(Other) faces that Day
Will be joyful,
Pleased with their Striving, –

In a Garden on high
Where they shall hear
No (word) of vanity:
Therein will be
A bubbling spring:
Therein will be Thrones
(Of dignity) raised on high,
Goblets placed (ready)
And Cushions set in rows,
And rich carpets
(All) spread out. (Q 88:8-16)

Q 56:8-38 gives more details, including the following:

Round about them will (serve)
Youths of perpetual (freshness),
With goblets, (shining) beakers,
And cups (filled) out of
Clear-flowing fountains:
No after-ache will they
Receive therefrom, nor will they
Suffer intoxication:
And with fruits,
Any that they may select; –
And the flesh of fowls,
Any that they may desire.
And (there will be) Companions
With beautiful, big,
And lustrous eyes, –
Like unto Pearls
Well-guarded,

A Reward for the Deeds
Of their past (Life)...

We have created (their Companions)
Of special creation.
And made them
Virgin-pure (and undefiled), –
Beloved (by nature),
Equal in age.

5. *Resurrection and Judgment*

Eschatology forms a very large part of the teaching of
the Quran, especially in the early surahs which reflect
Muhammad's early preaching at Mecca. There are
lengthy accounts of the resurrection and judgment
in surahs 75; 81:1-19; 82; 83:4-21; 84.

When the stars
Fall, losing their lustre;
When the mountains vanish
(Like a mirage);
When the she-camels,
Ten months with young,
Are left untended;
When the wild beasts
Are herded together
(In human habitations);
When the oceans
Boil over with a swell;
When the souls
Are sorted out,

(Being joined, like with like);
When the female (infant),
Buried alive, is questioned –
For what crime
She was killed;
When the Scrolls
Are laid open;
When the World on High
Is unveiled;
When the Blazing Fire
Is kindled to fierce heat;
And when the Garden
Is brought near –
(Then) shall each soul know
What it has put forward. (Q 81:2-14)

6. Forgiveness

There is very little in the Quran about forgiveness in comparison with other subjects which are dealt with at length. From what is mentioned, it is clear that it is regarded as a quite arbitrary act of Allah which has little, if any, moral basis, and requires no act of redemption or reconciliation. The following are some of the few verses dealing with this subject:

For those who reject Allah,
Is a terrible Penalty: but
For those who believe
And work righteous deeds,
Is Forgiveness, and
A magnificent Reward. (Q 35:7)

Allah forgiveth not
that partners should be set up
With Him; but He forgiveth
Anything else to whom
He pleaseth. (Q 4:48)

Leaving aside the unpardonable sin of *shirk*, sins
are divided into great and little sins. The great sins
[*kabira*] originally included murder, adultery, diso-
bedience, usury, the neglect of Friday prayers or the
Ramadan fast, forgetting the Quran after reading
it, swearing falsely or by any other name than that
of Allah, the practice of magic, gambling, dancing,
and shaving the beard. Some of these are no longer
regarded as great sins. The little sins [*saghira*] include such offences as lying, deception, anger, lust
and so forth.

7. Predestination
Many traditions suggest that humans cannot be held
responsible for their actions. Teaching on predestination is very closely linked with teaching on forgiveness, appearing in such verses as:

For Allah leaves to stray
Whom He wills, and guides
Whom He wills. (Q 35:8)

The same sentiments are expressed in Q 6:39; 14:4;
74:31.

8. Prayer

The Muslim prays five times a day at set times. There is however no single verse in the Quran where all five prayer times are mentioned together. Prayer for the Muslim is much more of a religious exercise than prayer as the Christian knows it. It must be said in Arabic, and the same forms and words are used every time. The following are some of the Quranic verses referring to prayer:

> And establish regular prayers
> At the two ends of the day
> And at the approaches of the night:
> For those things that are good
> Remove those that are evil. (Q 11:114)

> When ye pass
> (Congregational) prayers,
> Celebrate Allah's praises,
> Standing, sitting down,
> Or lying down on your sides;
> But when ye are free
> From danger, set up
> Regular Prayers:
> For such prayers
> Are enjoined on Believers
> At stated times. (Q 4:103)

Ceremonial ablutions must precede prayer:

> O ye who believe!
> When ye prepare

For prayer, wash
Your faces, and your hands
(And arms) to the elbows;
Rub your heads (with water);
And (wash) your feet
To the ankles. (Q 5:6)

9. Freedom of worship

Freedom of worship is a subject where there is con-
tradictory teaching within the Quran. A frequently
quoted verse in favour of freedom of religion is: 'Let
there be no compulsion in religion' (Q 2:256).

On the other side of the argument Muslims are
exhorted to 'fight and slay the pagans wherever ye
find them' (Q 9:5) and to 'fight those who believe
not in Allah nor the Last Day ... nor acknowledge the
Religion of Truth, from among the People of the Book,
until they pay the *jizya* with willing submission and
feel themselves subdued' (Q 9:29).

Since surah 9 post-dates surah 2, the rule of
abrogation indicates that it is surah 9 which should
be followed. This was certainly the practice of early
Muslims as they forcefully spread the new faith by
means of jihad. It is fortunate that this attitude is
only found in a minority of Muslims today. Nevertheless there are tragic examples of large-scale forced
conversions to Islam in recent history. In the early
twentieth century some 1.5 million Armenian and
other eastern Christians were massacred by the Turks.
In the early twenty-first century many thousands of
Indonesian Christians have been forced to convert to

Islam by 'jihad warriors' of many nationalities; any who refused were killed.

In connection with the subject of freedom of worship, it is important to remember also the Shariah's ruling that even if non-Muslim minorities are protected (i.e. not killed) and allowed to worship in their own way, they are still not granted equal rights with Muslims. (See *dhimmi*, page 20)

10. Islam is the only religion acceptable to God

If anyone desires
A religion other than
Islam (submission to Allah),
Never will it be accepted
Of him; and in the Hereafter
He will be in the ranks
Of those who have lost
(All spiritual good). (Q 3:85)

FOUR

THE FIVE PILLARS OF ISLAM

Introduction

Islam has a very highly developed code of religious observance, usually referred to as *arkan-ud-din* [pillars of religion]. This chapter describes the normal practices of the greater majority of Muslims; variations apply in some Muslim sects. These five pillars are:

Confessing the faith
Prayer
Fasting
Giving of alms
Pilgrimage to Mecca

Some Muslims add jihad as a sixth pillar.

All these are obligatory duties based on explicit injunctions in either the Quran or the hadith. There is no evading them. These aside, there are other duties which a good Muslim is expected to carry out, but while judged to be 'necessary', they are not, like the others, 'obligatory'.

Supreme importance is attached to these duties by most Muslims. They believe, on the authority of the Quran, that salvation is by 'works' such as these. Hence their concern, even anxiety and fear, to fulfil their duties. The representation of a pair of scales on the walls of Muslim buildings conveys to them more than the idea of justice. Those scales remind them of the statement in the Quran:

> Then those whose balance
> (Of good deeds) is heavy –
> They will attain salvation:
> But those whose balance
> Is light, will be those
> Who have lost their souls;
> In Hell they will abide. (Q 23:102,103)

Confessing the faith *[shahada]*

Shahada [confession] – derives from an Arabic root which yields the meaning 'testify', so that, strictly speaking, a Muslim's confession of faith takes the form:

'I testify that there is no god but Allah; I testify to His Unity and that He has no partner; I testify that Muhammad is His servant and His messenger.' Alternatively, the testimony may be made more briefly in the words of the *kalima*.

Prayer *[salah]*

1. Clothing

Clothing worn at a time of prayer is important to a Muslim, as the forehead must touch the ground. Muslim men wear brimless hats, (e.g. the fez) or turbans. In traditional clothing, the man normally removes his trousers under his long robes to pray and all Muslims remove their shoes. Western clothes are traditionally considered unfitting for a true Muslim.

2. Ablutions

Before a Muslim proceeds to pray, certain prescribed ceremonial ablutions must be performed. These are of three kinds.

(a) *wudu* – the lesser ablution. This is the most common form wherever water is available, and is customary before the appointed daily prayers.

Precise rules are prescribed for the washing of four parts of the body: the face, from the top of the forehead to the chin and as far as each ear; the hands and arms, up to the elbows; a fourth part of the head is rubbed with the wet hand; and the feet are washed up to the ankles. Members of the Shiah sect follow a different tradition and merely wipe – or rather rub – the feet.

Many Muslims believe that, should any of these parts of the body be left unwashed, then the subsequent prayers, though correctly recited, are robbed of all value. Nor is the due performance of such ablutions quite so simple as would appear to be the case. Bound up with the four main rules are no less than fourteen minor ones, all based on the *sunna* [custom] – of Muhammad himself. These include: to utter one of the names of *Allah* at the commencement of the ablutions; to clean one's teeth; to rinse out the mouth three times; to put water in the nostrils three times (the reason given for this particular injunction being a remark alleged to have been made by Muhammad about those who wake up from sleep, namely that 'Satan takes up his abode in the nose'); and to observe the proper order in washing the various parts of the head and body. The beard must be combed with wet fingers; one must rub under and between the toes with the wet fingers of the left hand, commencing with the toes of the right foot and finishing with the toes of the left foot.

It is an orthodox Muslim's confident belief, based on a saying attributed to Muhammad, that his little sins will be forgiven after such ablutions, duly followed by prayer

(b) *ghusl* – the bathing of the entire body after certain legal defilements, which need not be detailed here. In this case, water must be poured three times over the right shoulder, three times over the left, and finally, three times on the head. Besides this, there are three more 'obligatory' regulations: the mouth must be rinsed, water must be put in the nostrils, and the entire body must be washed. Not one hair should be left dry in the process.

(c) *tayammum* – purification by sand or earth. This procedure is prescribed to meet special circumstances; for instance, when water is not procurable within a distance of two miles, or when one is sick and the use of water might prove dangerous, or when water cannot be obtained without the risk of encountering an enemy, a wild beast or a reptile. Again, it may be resorted to by any person who, delayed by some festival or funeral, has insufficient time for the necessary ablutions. This cleansing is carried out by striking the sand or earth with one's open hands and then rubbing them over the face and arms up to the elbow.

3. The recitation of prayers

Having performed the necessary ablutions, the worshipper is now ready to proceed to the recitation of the prescribed prayers. These may be said in private or in public, and it is a common sight to see Muslim men, singly or in ranks, saying their prayers in the street and other public places, if they happen to be there when the time is due. But prayers said along with a congregation in a mosque are judged to be more meritorious.

The person of the worshipper, and their clothes, must be clean (hence the ablutions), and their face turned towards the *qibla* [direction of prayer], i.e. towards Mecca. There is a *mihrab*, or niche, in the wall of each mosque which indicates this direction.

4. The call to prayer

Prayer in a mosque is preceded by the *adhan* [call to prayer]. This call is chanted, in penetrating tones, by the muezzin from high up in a minaret of the mosque. It is common to use loudspeakers for amplification today. The call sounds forth five times a day, and is composed of short sentences which elicit similarly worded 'responses', sentence by sentence, from worshippers within hearing who intend to say their prayers. The muezzin calls out: 'Allah is great. I confess that there is no Allah but Allah. I testify Muhammad is the Apostle of Allah. Come to prayer; come to do good.' Early in the morning he calls, 'Prayer is better than sleep. Allah is great. There is no Allah but Allah.'

5. *Postures in prayer*

During the course of the prayer, certain postures are assumed and genuflections made by the worshipper in accordance with detailed rules. The actual words of these prayers are a recitation, in Arabic, of some passages of the Quran, mainly the very short chapters, placed in the canonical Quran at the close of the book, together with the *fatiha*, the name given to surah 1. To close the eyes during prayers would meet with the disapproval of the orthodox.

At prescribed intervals during such recitation, the worshipper utters the *takbir* [ascription of greatness to Allah], i.e. the well-known words, *Allahu Akbar* – 'Allah is great'. There immediately follows a lowly prostration, in a kneeling position, until the forehead actually touches the ground.

A certain number of set portions constitutes one complete recitation, and a worshipper may offer two or more such *rakaat* [units of prayer], according to whatever may have been his previously declared intention, said on hearing the call to prayer.

At the conclusion of these *rakaat* the worshipper offers the *durud*, or prayer for Muhammad, which runs: 'O Allah, have mercy on Muhammad and on his descendants. Thou art to be praised and Thou art great', etc. He then turns his head, first to the right and repeats the *salam*, or salutation: 'The peace and mercy of Allah be with you', then to the left with the same words. It is not certain to whom this salutation is addressed.

A noteworthy gesture marks the conclusion of the prayer. Raising the hands shoulder high, with palms upturned to heaven, the worshipper offers up a final supplication, either in Arabic or using his customary vocabulary, and then draws his hands down over his face and on to his breast as if to suggest that he is conveying the asked-for blessing to every part of his body.

6. *The times of prayer*

Tradition, not the Quran, has fixed the number of obligatory daily prayers as five. These are named and defined as follows:

> *fajr* – at dawn, before sunrise
> *zuhr* – soon after mid-day
> *asr* – mid-afternoon
> *maghrib* – soon after sunset
> *isha* – after nightfall.

The prayers on Friday [*jumma* – the Muslim holy day] take the place of the customary mid-day prayer. They differ in being preceded by an address (*khutba*) delivered by the *imam* [mosque leader].

7. Voluntary petitions [dua]
These are personal supplications to request help of various kinds according to the situation. They do not follow any set ritual or pattern.

Fasting [sawm]

Fasting is mainly practised during the days of the ninth month, Ramadan. This is generally believed to commemorate the occasion when Muhammad received his initial revelation from the angel Gabriel. Fasting is defined as abstinence from food and drink, perfumes, tobacco, and conjugal relations, during the hours between sunrise and sunset. Meals are to be taken at night. A person intending to keep the fast says: 'O Lord, I intend to fast tomorrow for Thy sake. Forgive my past and future sins.'

Each day, as soon as the sun has set, the Muslim breaks his fast with a very light meal, called *iftar*. Frequently a date is eaten, or a little water is drunk. A prayer is said: 'O Allah, I fasted for Thy sake and had faith in Thee, and confided in Thee, and now I break the fast with the food Thou givest. Accept this act.'

It is an obligatory duty to fast during the month of Ramadan. Young children and the mentally disabled are excused, while the sick, those on a journey, pregnant women and nursing mothers may postpone it to another time. The aged and infirm must, in lieu of fasting, feed a poor person. There are other fasts also, such as that on 10th Muharram (commemorating a key day in the creation), but these are voluntary.

The fast of Ramadan begins with the first sighting of the new moon, marking the opening of the month, and is rigidly kept. When the month of Ramadan falls in the heat of a tropical summer, or in the long summer days of the high latitudes, the fast can be a severe trial. However, Muslim employers do not usually expect much work from their employees during Ramadan. There is exuberant feasting each evening after sunset, and a joyful celebration at the end of the month (*id-ul-fitr*).

Certain acts render the fast invalid: if, when cleaning the teeth, a drop of water should pass down the throat; if food is eaten under compulsion; if medicine is put into the ear, nose, or even a wound in the head; if a meal has been taken on the erroneous supposition that it was night-time; if after the night meal a portion of food larger than a grain of corn should remain between the teeth or in a cavity of a tooth; if food is vomited. In all such cases another day's fast must be kept. Where the fast is wilfully broken, certain alternative penalties are prescribed. It used to be that the delinquent had to atone by setting free a slave, or by fasting every day for two months, or by giving sixty persons two meals each, or one person twice-daily meals for sixty days. Even now imprisonment and fines are enforced in certain countries.

Giving of alms *[zaka]*

In Islam, two terms are used for almsgiving: *zaka*, obligatory alms due – subject to certain conditions – from every Muslim; and *sadaqa*, voluntary offerings, made at the time of the annual festival known as *id-ul-fitr*, at the end of Ramadan. This second term may be used of alms in general. It will suffice here to consider only *zaka*.

It is an obligatory duty for every Muslim of full age to give *zaka* in proportion to his property, provided he has sufficient for his own subsistence. The conditions which make *zaka* incumbent upon one are that a person should be free, sane, adult and a Muslim, and the possessor of the statutory amount of property. In Sunni Islam the rate is 2.5 per cent.

Zaka is to be presented to certain classes of persons, which included not only the poor and needy but also those in debt, travellers, those who administered the funds and recent converts to Islam. They could also be used for 'the cause of Allah', a phrase which encompasses jihad (Q 9:60). *Zaka*, from the beginning, could be given to a believing slave to enable him to purchase his freedom, or to enable a poor person to undertake the hajj. But *zaka* must not be used for the building of mosques, funeral expenses, or the liquidation of debts of a deceased person; neither is it permitted to give it to parents or grandparents, children or grandchildren. These prohibitions are often not observed today.

Pilgrimage to Mecca *[hajj]*

This also is an obligatory duty, as enjoined in the Quran:

> And proclaim the Pilgrimage
> Among men . . .
> Then let them complete
> The rites prescribed
> For them, perform their vows,
> And (again) circumambulate
> The Ancient House. (Q 22:27-29)

Another passage concerning this 'house', i.e., the Kaba, called 'the house of God', reads:

> Pilgrimage thereto is a duty
> Men owe to Allah, –
> Those who can afford
> The journey ... (Q 3:97)

A well-known commentator declared the words 'can afford' were interpreted by Muhammad himself to mean the possession of food for the journey, and an animal to ride on. Some traditions permit the sending of a substitute, even posthumously.

Muhammad is alleged to have declared that it is only necessary for a believer to make the pilgrimage once in his lifetime; any additional pilgrimages to the holy city are 'voluntary'. If a child makes the pilgrimage he must go again on coming of age. This pilgrimage must be made in the twelfth month, Dhul Hijjah.

The precincts of the Kaba at Mecca are hallowed as the supposed scene of Hagar's distress for her son Ishmael. According to some legends, Abraham and Ishmael established the pilgrimage to Arafat, culminating with the sacrifice at Mina in remembrance of the sacrifice made by Abraham.

There are very intricate rules laid down for the performance of the pilgrimage, which vary between different schools of Islamic law. Some parts are obligatory, others are merely 'necessary'. At the heart of the rites is the ceremony of walking seven times round the Kaba. This seven-fold circumambulation is called the *tawaf*. The pilgrims dress in white.

During the circumambulation of the Kaba, the pilgrim is expected to kiss the Black Stone. This is the most venerated object in the ancient shrine. It is probably a meteorite, and from of old has been treated with awe as something that fell from the sky. According to one tradition, Muhammad said: 'The Black Stone came down from paradise. It was whiter than milk, but the sins of the children of Adam have made it black [i.e. through kissing it].'

If the crowd is so large that the pilgrim cannot get near enough to kiss, he or she must touch it with their hand, or with a staff, and kiss that which has been in contact with the stone. At this time the pilgrim says, 'O Allah, I do this in Thy belief and in verification of Thy book and in pursuance of Thy prophet's example. May Allah bless and preserve him! O accept Thou my supplication, diminish my obstacles, pity my humiliation, and graciously grant me Thy pardon.'

Over a period of several days various other sacred places are visited in a certain order, including Mount Arafat and the valley of Mina. At Mina, stones are thrown at three pillars, one of which symbolizes the devil. At the end animals are sacrificed, and the male pilgrim shaves his head. Henceforth he is known and respected as a 'hajji' or 'hadji', one who has made the pilgrimage to Mecca.

Subsequently, most pilgrims make the *ziyara* or visit to the tomb of Muhammad at Medina.

The entire set of ceremonies connected with the hajj were taken over by Muhammad, with very little change, from pre-Islamic paganism.

FIVE

WOMEN IN ISLAM

A woman's place in the family

Muslim women are always under the protection of a male relative: father, husband, brother, uncle or son. Many of the restrictions on a woman are due to the need for her honour – on which the honour of the whole family depends – to be carefully preserved. It will be argued that the more strictly she is controlled, the more highly she is valued. It is essential for a girl to be a virgin at marriage.

A woman will often need permission from a male relative even to visit her mother or sisters. She will seldom go out alone, but usually with a close male relative or a number of female relatives. Even young children can chaperone their mothers or elder sisters in this way.

The woman's place is in the home. Her role is to produce sons for her husband, to care for them, and to do the housework. Some women may go out to work to add to the family's finances, but this is usually only in cases of necessity. The husband will rarely assist with the housework, even if his wife has a full-time job. Although the wife normally does the cooking, in some societies the husband will cook for special occasions.

Since women are so much at home they usually welcome visits, provided the visitor is female. In the West a good time to visit a Muslim woman is in the early afternoon, when the chores are done and the children not yet home from school. Alternatively the early evening, when the children may have gone to their Quran school and the husband is still out at work.

When mixed groups are visiting, the women of the family will often stay in an inner room while the men entertain the male visitors and the less well known female visitors. A female Christian visitor may often find herself put in this mixed-sex room, away from the women of the family. To be invited to join the women in the inner family room is a compliment which indicates intimacy and trust.

Clothing

Islam teaches that a woman must dress modestly, covering herself from neck to wrist and ankle as well as covering her hair. Different cultures fulfil these criteria in different ways. The covering should be opaque and loose-fitting. Long, loose hair is considered immodest.

In some parts of the world, further demands are placed by custom on the woman, for example, covering the feet, hands or face. In some cultures, though brightly-coloured clothes may be worn in the home, these must be covered with a dark outer garment when going out.

The *hijab* – the woman's veil and head-covering – can have political significance. In some more secular countries, such as Turkey, it is banned in certain contexts. In conservative countries, such as Saudi Arabia, it is obligatory. In the West it can be a point of controversy where Muslim girls may be disallowed from wearing it to school, or Muslim women forbidden to wear it at work. Many young Muslim women have adopted the *hijab* in recent years both in the West and elsewhere. Sometimes it is because of family pressure, but sometimes by their own choice through religious conviction.

Marriage

Marriage is seen in the Quran as a gift from God (Q 16:72) and the normal human condition (Q 4:25). Singleness is viewed as very undesirable and probably an indication of immorality. Likewise voluntary childlessness is a completely baffling concept to most Muslims. An older Christian woman who is single will find herself having to answer many questions from Muslim friends about her strange position in society. There are, however, a few sections of Muslim society where celibacy for religious reasons is approved.

Marriage is not so much a joining of the two individuals involved as a joining of their respective families. As such, marriages are almost always arranged by the families concerned, with little or no consultation with the young couple, who sometimes do not even see each other until the wedding day. Strictly speaking, the young person is allowed to refuse the prospective marriage partner whom their family chooses for them, but in practice there is often enormous pressure and emotional blackmail put on them to accept and not disgrace their family by refusing. The bride is not necessarily even present at the marriage contract ceremony, but can be represented by a male relative.

It is common in some societies for marriages to be arranged with close relatives, for example, first and second cousins. If the marriage is arranged outside the family, then factors such as financial situation and social status are very important in making the choice. A Muslim man is permitted to marry a Christian or Jewish woman, but a Muslim woman can only marry a Muslim man.

Love is expected to grow between husband and wife after their marriage, rather than before. Even so, this love is not usually expected to blossom into the kind of devotion and tender companionship which westerners generally hope for in marriage. A Muslim girl is taught from childhood to look to her children, especially her sons, for love rather than to her husband, who is primarily the provider and protector. Generally the closest bond in a Muslim family is between mother and son.

For young Muslims who have grown up in a western society there can be a very painful conflict between the ideals of the older generations in the family and the ideals of society as a whole. It is common in Britain for a spouse to be found and brought over from the 'home country', so that husband and wife almost inevitably come to the marriage with radically different expectations.

However, many Muslim families in the West nowadays relax the rules somewhat. For example, they may allow the young couple to spend a few hours talking together before they must decide whether to get married. The happiest young couples are probably those whose 'love match' is approved by their respective families, who will then take over and make the usual arrangements and negotiations with each other.

Although both families and the groom will rejoice over the coming marriage, the bride is not necessarily expected to do so in a traditionally arranged marriage. She will be leaving her family to live with a strange family she does not know. A smiling bride is considered improper in some societies, and tears (of sadness, not joy) are required to show how much she will miss her family.

It is a terrible disgrace for an unhappy wife to leave her husband. Her own family – who would share her disgrace – will do all they can to prevent her returning to them, no matter how badly she is being treated by her husband or in-laws.

A Muslim man is permitted to have up to four wives at the same time, though he is required to treat them all equally. He is also permitted to beat a disobedient wife (Q 4:34).

Divorce

According to the Shariah, it is easy for a Muslim man to divorce his wife; he need only say to her three times in front of witnesses: 'I divorce you.' On the other hand, it is very difficult for a woman to divorce her husband.

The children of a marriage belong to the husband and his family. Whether the wife is divorced or widowed, she must hand over the children (though she can keep babies until she has finished breast-feeding them, which is supposed to be at the age of two).

Divorce in the early years of a marriage is frowned on, though many Muslims consider it less disgraceful if the marriage has lasted some time. By the same token, breaking an engagement is often considered to be even more disgraceful than divorce.

In Shiah Islam there is the possibility of temporary marriages called *muta*. The length of the marriage is agreed in the marriage contract, and can vary from one hour to ninety-nine years.

Family planning and abortion

Although large families are generally sought after, contraception is not forbidden in Islam. Abortion is permitted only if the mother's life is in danger or if there is a strong possibility that the baby will be severely disabled.

Because all the children of a Muslim man are considered Muslims, whatever the religion of the mother, deliberately fathering many Muslim children has been one of the ways in which Islam has been spread at certain times and places. This mindset is apparently behind the widespread rape of Christian women by Muslim men that happens today in some Muslim countries. It should be noted that rape is also considered to dishonour the woman.

Spiritual duties

Women are required to practise the five pillars of Islam, as men are, though menstruation is considered to invalidate prayer and fasting. Muslim societies vary as to whether women are expected to attend public prayers in the mosque. Even if they are, they will do so in a secluded place, separate from and invisible to the men. They are promised the same heavenly reward (Q 16:97), though it has to be said that a paradise full of beautiful virgins (Q 44:54; 55:72) would not seem to be as great a delight for women as for men. Several ahadith state that a woman's obedience to her husband is the main prerequisite for her to get to heaven.

Many women have little knowledge of true Islam or the teachings of the Quran, though they generally know all about the day of judgment. Often they are familiar with certain ahadith which indicate that most women will go to hell (though most men will go to heaven). It is hardly surprising that their lives are often dominated by superstition and fear, and many practise 'folk Islam', seeking help from the Muslim saints – living and dead – and protection against evil spirits and the evil eye. They use talismans, charms, amulets, spells and curses to try to achieve their aims.

Legal status

The Shariah generally gives women only half the value of men in terms of testimony and compensation. Thus two female witnesses would equal one male witness in an Islamic law court (where verdicts are arrived at primarily by counting the number of witnesses on each side). The same injury sustained by a man and by a woman will usually result in compensation for the woman at 50 per cent of what the man receives. Similarly, a daughter generally inherits only half what her brother does; this is justified by the greater financial responsibilities of men.

The unequal position of women as regards divorce and polygamy has already been mentioned.

SIX

SUNNI AND SHIAH

Islam has two main divisions: Sunni and Shiah. Sunni Muslims form the majority (about 90%), and this booklet has mainly described Sunni beliefs and practices. Shiah Muslims are a majority only in Iran, Iraq, Azerbaijan and Bahrain. In some places they are persecuted by Sunnis.

Origins of Shiah Islam

The split into Sunni and Shiah originated in a dispute over the leadership succession little more than twenty years after Muhammad's death. Muhammad's successors were known as caliphs, and the first three have already been mentioned (see page 13). The fourth caliph, who succeeded in 656, was Ali, the husband of Muhammad's daughter Fatima. He was not universally accepted as the rightful successor and Muslims began to fight each other over this issue. Ali was eventually murdered in 661 and the struggle was continued by his two sons, Hassan and Hussain. Hassan was poisoned in about 670 and Hussain died at the Battle of Karbala in 680. Ali's followers, Shiah Ali [the party of Ali], became the Shiah Muslims.

Shiah beliefs

Shiahs believe that Ali was the first legitimate imam (their preferred word for 'caliph') and reject the first three. They greatly revere him and his sons, their main annual festival being a commemoration of the martyrdom of Hussain on 10th Muharram. This day is marked with passion plays, wailing and flagellation. Shiahs believe that only Ali's descendants, who through Fatima are also descendants of Muhammad, can be imams. They consider these imams to be infallible and sinless.

Shiahs add two more key beliefs to the five pillars of Islam: the importance of the imamate and that justice is part of God's nature. Their practice of temporary marriages has already been mentioned. Shiahs hold that *ijtihad* [logical deduction] may still be practised, i.e. that parts of the Shariah can be adapted. By contrast most Sunnis believe that the Shariah can never be changed.

Sub-divisions of Shiah Islam

Shiahs have split into many different sects. Amongst the most well known are the Ismailis, led by the Agha Khan. Both the Druzes and the Bahais also originated from Shiah Islam, though they have diverged so far from it that they are no longer considered to be Muslims.

The largest sub-division of Shiahs are called the 'Twelvers'. They acknowledge twelve imams, the first being Ali and the twelfth being a four-year-old boy who disappeared into a cave near Baghdad in 873. The twelfth imam, called 'the hidden imam', is believed to be still alive and exerting a spiritual influence on his followers. He will return as the Mahdi [rightly guided one], and establish Islamic rule throughout the world.

Taqiya [Dissimulation]

Perhaps the most important feature of Shiah Islam which a Christian who is building a friendship with a Shiah Muslim should be aware of is the practice of *taqiya* [dissimulation]. Shiah Islam allows its followers to lie and deceive and deny what they really believe, so long as they continue to adhere to the belief in their hearts. The tenth century Shiah divine, Ibn Babuya al-Saquq, stated, 'Our belief concerning *taqiya* is that it is obligatory ... God has described the showing of friendship to unbelievers' as being possible only 'in the state of *taqiya*'.

Although the doctrine of *taqiya* is generally considered to have developed because of the persecution of Shiahs by Sunnis, some Muslims assert that *taqiya* is also legitimate in Sunni Islam. There are a number of ahadith which indicate that lying is permitted in the following three situations: (1) a man may lie to his wife to please her, (2) to bring reconciliation between two parties who have quarrelled, (3) in war, espionage etc.

SEVEN

SUFISM - ISLAMIC MYSTICISM

The Sufis are the mystics of Islam and can belong to almost any group or sect except probably the Wahabis and Ahmadis, who condemn the practice of visiting the shrines of holy people. It attracts followers from a wide range of intellectual and social backgrounds. The most famous Sufi leader was the Persian, Al Ghazali (1058 – 1111).

The movement began with ascetics who sought to escape the world and live in austere simplicity, calm and passivity. Poverty and purity were their hallmarks. One of these ascetics in the eighth century took to wearing a woollen robe, and this may be the origin of the name 'Sufi', from the Arabic word for 'wool'. Alternatively, it could be derived from *safu*, the Arabic for 'purity'.

Central to Sufism is the desire for a personal loving relationship with God and a feeling of closeness to Him, resulting ultimately in union with God. This longing is expressed in many beautiful love poems. The methods used to try to achieve such union include meditation, contemplation and the tireless repetition of one or another of Allah's names. This repetition is called *dhikr* [remembering God] and its purpose is to induce a trance. The Muslim rosary [*tasbih*] is also used. One of the Sufi brotherhoods, the Maulawiya, who originated in Turkey, use a rapid rotating dance to enter into a trance, and are sometimes called the 'whirling dervishes'.

Sufism was often controversial. Even in the early days Sufis were condemned by many Muslims because their practices and even their clothes seemed to have been derived from Christian hermits and monks of the time. The fact that they also abandoned certain Islamic prohibitions from time to time, for example, drinking alcohol, also brought condemnation on their heads from some orthodox Muslims.

Among Sufis the distinction between male and female tends to disappear. Some women even became revered saints and religious leaders. Many women follow Sufi saints today. Some become disciples of a chosen spiritual leader, though proper initiation is generally reserved for men. Many women go with their menfolk on pilgrimages to shrines, particularly to celebrate the birth or the death of the saint and to secure his help with health and family problems.

The Sufis were great missionaries, active in bringing Islam to the Mongols and Central Asia in particular.

The Sufi's longing to know God personally, and His love, is an obvious starting point from which the Christian Gospel could be shared.

EIGHT

THE 'GOSPEL' OF BARNABAS

A Christian discussing matters of faith with a Muslim may find their friend alluding to the 'Gospel of Barnabas'. This document is believed by many Muslims to contain the ultimate truth about the life and teaching of Jesus. Some even hold that it is the true and original *Injil*, for which Christians later substituted the New Testament.

The book professes to be a gospel written by the Apostle Barnabas. The author also claims that he, Barnabas, was one of the twelve disciples of Jesus, for which there is no support in the real Gospels. Furthermore, his denunciation of the Apostle Paul's teachings discounts the close and supportive relationship which existed between Paul and Barnabas according to the New Testament. The book denies that Jesus is the Son of God and portrays Him as a fore-runner (like John the Baptist) who proclaimed the future coming of Muhammad. It also denies the crucifixion. In addition, it even contradicts the Quran by declaring that Muhammad will be the Messiah, whereas the Gospels and Quran agree that this title belongs to Jesus alone. Such evidence, along with geographical and historical errors, shows that the Barnabas of the New Testament is not the author of this book.

Various references in the 'Gospel of Barnabas' point to its having been written in the Middle Ages, not earlier than the fourteenth century, i.e. well over a thousand years after Christ and 700 years after Muhammad. The book contains most of the stories found in the four Gospel accounts in the New Testament, but with many things artfully turned in favour of Islam. A general study of its contents and authorship shows that it is a clumsy attempt to forge a life of Jesus consonant with the profile of Him in the Quran and Islamic tradition.

An English translation of the 'Gospel of Barnabas' by Lonsdale and Laura Ragg was reprinted in Pakistan in the 1970s and circulated in large numbers.

For further reading see John Gilchrist's *Origins and Sources of the Gospel of Barnabas*.

Nine

Sharing the Gospel with Muslims

Islam – which now claims a billion adherents – is without doubt the greatest single challenge facing the Church today. Having emerged from the shame of western colonization, and funded with oil wealth from the Middle East, Muslims have become a confident people, eager to make converts, whether by force, persuasion or material inducements. Where they are present as minorities in the West, Muslims are vocal in asserting their rights and assiduous in working for freedoms and privileges which are not granted to non-Muslims in Muslim-majority contexts. Despite divisions within Islam, Muslims have a basic unity and loyalty to each other which takes priority over all other loyalties. Excellent international networking and use of the most advanced communications technology reinforces the theology behind this. For Christians who would preach the Gospel to Muslims, nothing less than the power of God released by the Holy Spirit is adequate.

Most Muslims who come to Christ are not won over by intellectual arguments which disprove the validity of Islam. Rather they have a personal encounter

with Christ. Often this happens by reading the New
Testament. Others have testified to the power of the
love of Christ working through their Christian friends.
Sometimes the Lord will call a Muslim to Himself
through dreams and visions.

However, a knowledge of Islam can equip Christians to counter some of the most frequent objections
raised by Muslims. These have been covered in
the preceding sections, and include the belief that
Christians worship three gods, that 'Son of God' is
a physical description, and that the Christians have
corrupted their Scriptures. A knowledge of Islam can
also oil the wheels of the conversation and encourage
a Muslim to investigate Christianity just as his or
her Christian friend has clearly spent time learning
about Islam.

The Christian seeking to witness to Muslims
should have a thorough knowledge of the Bible, as well
as of Islam. Personal testimony is always powerful.

For the Muslim, Muhammad is the last and greatest of the prophets. No useful purpose is served by
unnecessary criticism of him. Nothing more readily
provokes a fanatical outburst than an attack on his
character. Muslims usually add respectful honorifics
when they mention the name 'Muhammad'. While a
Christian cannot with integrity use these, the phrase
'your prophet Muhammad' may be a helpful one, po-
lite but without conceding any belief in the validity of
Muhammad's prophethood. Another possibility would
be 'the founder of Islam' [bani-e-Islam], a phrase often
used by Muslims. When challenged as to the life and

work of Muhammad and the authority and inspiration of the Quran, it may be wiser to attempt to bring the questioner to consider Christ rather than to counter the Muslims' claims about Muhammad, and to point to the Bible rather than to become involved in argument about the nature of the Quran.

It is important to bear in mind that Muslims are individuals. Your Muslim friend may be a nominal Muslim who does little more than keep Ramadan in a half-hearted way and lives in fear of going to hell. He or she may know less about orthodox Islam than you do. Women in particular are often very ill taught in their faith, and follow a folk Islam of superstition and occultic activities that has little to do with real Islam. Your Muslim friend may be very westernized, liberal and open to change. Equally he or she may be an extremist who would like to see the establishment of an Islamic state ruled by Shariah. London (like certain other European capitals) is home to many Islamic extremists who have been exiled from their own Muslim countries for terrorism. Your Muslim friend may be cultivating a friendship with you in order to try to convert you to Islam. Mission [*dawa*] is just as much an obligation for the Muslim believer as for the Christian believer and they use all the same methods.

If you are a white Christian and you are seeking to witness to non-white Muslims, you have a disadvantage in that many Muslims think that all white people are Christians and judge Christianity on the basis of the godless immorality so sadly evident in

western society. The Christian believer must make it
clear that true Christians are just as shocked by this
as Muslims. In order to help prove this, the Christian
must be very careful about certain aspects of culture.
Clothes should be modest and not close-fitting, especially for women. The Christian should only seek to
talk to those of the same sex. Any conversation with
the opposite sex should be at the Muslim's initiative.
Never touch anyone of the opposite sex, even to shake
hands, unless the other person initiates it. Try also
to avoid eye contact with the opposite sex, even if a
conversation develops. Treat both the Bible and the
Quran with great respect, not placing them on the
floor and not writing in them.

On the other hand being white can open doors. A
friendship with a white person is a complete novelty
to some Muslims, especially older women confined
to the home, and this may act in your favour. You
may be able to help in practical ways with filling
in forms etc. and show love to your Muslim friend
like this. Also, younger Muslims in the West, who
live in western culture during school or work hours
and Muslim culture at home, may really appreciate
the friendship of someone who understands both the
cultures and can imagine the conflicts, frustrations
and stresses that result.

TEN

CARE OF CONVERTS

Care of converts, new and old, is vital, for the pressure on them is great.

Converts generally face rejection by their outraged family. There may be, for example, threats of violence or threats to withdraw financial support for a student. The convert is often expelled from the family home. A married convert will probably lose access to his or her children. There may be emotional blackmail; for example, the distraught mother says she will kill herself if her beloved child does not return to Islam. Sometimes this reaction is delayed until the convert is baptized.

The Church must become the convert's new family, and this means more than having a cup of tea together after the Sunday service. Practical provision and accommodation may be necessary, alongside supportive friendship. This is not a short-term thing. The rejection by family is a continuing source of pain if the breach cannot be healed.

Another difficulty facing new Christians from a Muslim background is the lack of a framework of rules in their new faith. Islam is so thoroughly regulated, with rules even about which direction to lie in bed and special prayers to say when going to the lavatory, that a new convert can be left feeling in desperate need of guidance about how to live as a Christian. Discipleship training is essential, as soon as possible.

A practical difficulty for single converts is finding a marriage partner. For those brought up in a faith where marriages are arranged by parents, courting can be very difficult. In some churches, converts are also treated with suspicion, and even referred to still as 'Muslim'. It may sometimes be necessary for the church leadership to take on the role of discreetly finding a Christian marriage partner.

GLOSSARY OF ISLAMIC TERMS

adhan the call to prayer

al-adha   the pilgrims' sacrifice in the valley of *mina* near Mecca

ahl-al-kitab   people of the book (i.e. Jews and Christians)

Ahmadis   also 'Ahmadiyyas'; an unorthodox Muslim sect from Pakistan/India, proscribed in some Muslim countries

arkan-ud-din   the pillars of religion

asr   the afternoon prayer (third prayer time of the day)

ayah   literally 'sign'; verse of the Quran. The Urdu word is *ayat*.

Ayatollah   literally 'sign of Allah'; term of honour for religious leader in Shiah Islam

bani-e-Islam   the founder of Islam, i.e. Muhammad

basi bad al-maut   resurrection after death

begum   Urdu word for a respected, married woman

bismillah   in the name of Allah

burqa   Urdu term for clothing that envelops a woman in public, covering her whole body and face

Caliph	in Arabic *khalifah*; successor, vice-regent, the leader of the whole Muslim community worldwide
chador	large cloth covering a woman's head and body in public as used in Iran
Dajjal	the Antichrist
dawa	mission, in the sense of making converts
dhikr	literally 'remembrance'; the invocation of God by repetition of one of his names
dhimmi	non-Muslims in an Islamic society, subjugated people, treated as second-class
din	religion, in its practice
dua	voluntary petitions in prayer
durud	prayer for Muhammad
fajr	dawn; the dawn prayer (first prayer time of the day)
fard	obligatory
fatiha	the first surah of the Quran
fatwa	a published decision concerning religious doctrine or law
fiqh	literally 'understanding'; the science of law, jurisprudence
firman	edict, command, decree
ghusl	bathing the entire body
hadith	tradition or report of a precedent set by
(pl. ahadith)	Muhammad or his early followers
hajj	the annual pilgrimage to Mecca, to be performed by the believer

	once in a lifetime if economically possible
hajji or hadji	one who has made the pilgrimage to Mecca
hijab	literally 'partition' or 'curtain'; the institution of the seclusion of women; often used to mean the woman's head covering which conceals, neck, hair and sometimes face
hijrah	Muhammad's flight from Mecca to Medina in A.D. 622, which was used as the starting point of the Islamic calendar
Iblis	one of the names of the devil
id-ul-adha	the feast of sacrifice observed seventy days after the end of the fast of Ramadan
id-ul-fitr	the feast that is observed when the fasting month of Ramadan is ended
iftar	the evening meal after each day's fast during Ramadan
ijma	consensus of opinion of the recognized religious authorities at any given time concerning the interpretation and application of the teaching of the Quran in any particular situation
ijtihad	literally 'exertion'; a logical deduction on a legal or theological question by a *mujtahid*, as distinguished from *ijma* which is a

collective opinion. Sunnis believe that 'the door of *ijithad* has closed', whereas Shiahs believe *ijtihad* can still be practised.

imam
: leader of a mosque. (In Shiah Islam 'imam' is the term used for the leader of the whole Muslim community worldwide.)

iman
: faith believed and confessed

Injil
: The revelation made by *Allah* to Jesus; the word occurs ten times in the Quran. Strictly speaking it refers to the Gospels only, but is sometimes applied to the whole New Testament.

isha
: the night prayer (the fifth prayer time of the day)

janna
: literally 'garden'; a term used for paradise

jihad
: literally 'an effort of striving'; a religious war; sometimes understood as spiritual struggle

jinn
: a spirit, created by Allah. There are some good jinn, but many are evil.

jizya
: tax payable by *dhimmi*, as a sign of their subjugation to Muslims

jumma
: Friday, the Muslim holy day

Kaba
: cube-shaped shrine at Mecca

kabira
: 'great' sins

kalima
: literally 'word'; Islamic creed

khutba
: address (sermon) at Friday mid-day prayers

kismat	it is my lot (an expression of fatalism)
kitab (pl. *kutub*)	book
maghrib	sunset, the evening prayer (fourth prayer time of the day)
Mahdi	literally 'rightly guided one', whose return is awaited by Shiah Muslims
maktub	it is written (an expression of fatalism)
malaikah	angels
maqdur	it is decided (an expression of fatalism)
marabout	a religious leader who exercises occult powers. The term is chiefly used in North and West Africa.
mihrab	niche in wall of mosque, indicating direction of prayer (towards Mecca)
miraj	miraculous night-time journey of Muhammad to heaven
mizan	scales on which good and bad deeds are weighed
muezzin	the one who gives out the call to prayer
Muharram	the first month of the Islamic year, when the death of Hussain is commemorated from 1st to 10th. Especially observed by Shiah Muslims
mujahed	one who goes on jihad; Islamic warrior
(pl. *mujahedin*)	

mujtahid	literally 'one who strives to obtain a high position and learning'; a very learned religious teacher, one who practices *ijtihad*
mullah	a religious teacher. The term is more common in Pakistan and India.
muta	literally 'enjoyment'; a marriage contracted for a limited time, e.g during a jihad or a pilgrimage; a feature of Shia Islam
nabi	prophet
pir	a holy man or saint
purda	literally 'curtain'; the seclusion of women
qara	read, recite
qibla	direction to which one turns in praying, i.e. towards Mecca
qiyas	analogous reasoning
Quran	the Muslims' holy book
rakah (pl. *rakaat*)	unit of ritual prayer
Ramadan	the ninth month in the Islamic calendar, the fasting month
rasul	apostle, messenger, one to whom an inspired book was revealed
riba	interest on money lent
sadaqa	voluntary offerings made at *id-ul-fitr*
saghira	'little' sins
salah	Muslim ritual prayer recited five times a day
salam	literally 'peace'; a word used as a

	greeting or salutation
sawm	the act of fasting
shahada	Islamic creed
Shariah	Islamic religious law. *Shariat* is the Urdu word.
Shaytan	one of the names of the devil
sheikh	elder, leader, chief
Shiah	the Muslim sect that believes that the rightful successor to Muhammad was Ali, his closest relative
shirk	associating anyone with Allah as a co-deity. The worst sin in Islam.
sirat	a very narrow bridge, spanning the fires of hell
Sufi	a mystic
sunna	literally 'a trodden path'; the customs of Muhammad and his early followers who knew him personally
Sunni	literally 'one of the path'; orthodox Islam; the majority, who follow the successors of Muhammad by election
surah	literally 'a row or series'; used exclusively for chapters of the Quran
takbir	ascription of greatness to Allah
talaq	A word used by a husband to divorce his wife. He must say it three times to her: 'I divorce you, I divorce you, I divorce you.'
taqdir	the doctrine of predestination
taqiya	literally 'guarding oneself'; a

	doctrine by which the Shiah justifies denying some of his or her religious belief in order to escape persecution, extended to permit lying in a variety of circumstances
tasbih	rosary
Taurah	the Torah, the law of Moses, the first five books of the Old Testament, 'taurat' in Urdu
tawaf	circumambulation of the Kaba seven times
tayammum	purification by sand or earth (when water is not procurable)
ulama	group of theologians
ummah	the whole community of Islam, the totality of all Muslims
Wahabis	members of a puritanical reform movement of Sunni Islam founded in the eighteenth century A.D. They are dominant today in Saudi Arabia.
wudu/wazu/wuzu	lesser ablution, as distinguished from *ghusl*
yawm al-akhirah	literally 'last day'; day of judgment
Zabur	Psalms
zaka	the legal alms due from every Muslim; *zakat* in Urdu
ziyara	a visit to Muhammad's tomb in Medina; has come to mean visits to the tomb of any Muslim saint
zuhr	the mid-day prayer (second prayer time of the day)

APPENDICES

APPENDIX I: A chronology of Muhammad's life

Scholars are unable to pinpoint many of the dates exactly. For example, Muhammad's birth is placed at 20 August 570 by Caussin de Perceval, 20 April 571 by Sprenger and by Mahmud Pasha Falki, and 22 April 571 in the following chronology. The latest research has suggested that most of the facts pertaining to Muhammad's life are shrouded in uncertainty. Muslims would suggest a chronology of Muhammad's life as follows:

Life at MECCA

Birth	12th Rabi al-awwal (Monday, 22 April, A.D. 571) Father, Abdullah, already dead.
Age 6	Death of mother, Aminah
Age 8	Death of grandfather, Abdul Mutalib
Age 12	First business trip to Syria
Age 25	Marriage to Khadijah
Age 40	Prophethood (A.D. 610)
1st year of prophethood	*Fajr* and *asr* prayers, two *rakaat* each
1st–3rd year	Secret preaching of Islam
At the end of 3rd year	Open call to Islam from Mount Safa, near Mecca
3rd–5th year	Hostility of Meccan infidels

5th year	Migration of Muslims to Abyssinia [Ethiopia]
6th year	Umar accepts Islam
7th–9th year	Continued hostility of Meccan infidels
10th year	Year of Sorrow – deaths of uncle, Abu Talib, and first wife, Khadijah
	Miraj [Muhammad's night journey to heaven], 27th Rajab
	Five times daily prayers made obligatory during *miraj*
13th year	Hijrah to Medina, 27th Safar (A.D 622)

Life at MEDINA

A.H. 1 (first year after the hijrah)	Arrival at Quba, 8th Rabi al-awwal
	Arrival at Medina
	Establishment of First Islamic State
	Treaty with the Jews
A.H. 2	Jihad ordained, 12th Safar
	Adhan and *zaka* introduced
	Revelation about the change of *qibla*, Monday, 15th Shaban
	Ramadan fast prescribed
	Id-ul-fitr, 1st Shawal
	Battle of Badr, 17th Ramadan
	Marriage of Ali and Fatimah, after Badr
A.H. 3	First revelation restricting the drinking of wine
	Battle of Uhud, 5th Shawal
	First revelation about *riba* (interest)

	Revelation of laws about orphans, after Uhud
	Revelation of laws of inheritance
	Revelation of laws about marriage and the rights of wives
A.H. 4	Revelation of the requirement for *hijab* for women
	Revelation about the prohibition on drinking wine
A.H. 5	Battle of Dumatul Jandal and battle of Banu al-Mustaliq
	Revelation of laws about adultery and slander
	Battle of Ahzab
A.H. 7	Letters to rulers of different countries including Persian and Roman emperors
	Battle of Khibar
	Revelation of laws about marriage and divorce
A.H. 8	Battle of Mutah
	Conquest of Mecca, 20th Ramadan
	Battle of Hunain
	Siege of Taif
	Revelation of final order prohibiting *riba*
A.H. 9	Battle of Tabuk
	Revelation of order concerning *jizya* tax for non-Muslim minorities
	Hajj prescribed

A.H. 10   Farewell address, 9th Dhul hijjah

A.H. 11   Death, 12th Rabi al-awwal, reputedly
                 at age 63 (A.D. 632)

APPENDIX II: Historical development of Islamic sects

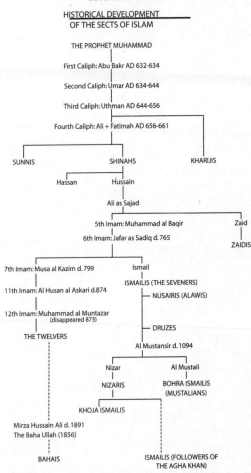

HISTORICAL DEVELOPMENT
OF THE SECTS OF ISLAM

THE PROPHET MUHAMMAD

First Caliph: Abu Bakr AD 632-634

Second Caliph: Umar AD 634-644

Third Caliph: Uthman AD 644-656

Fourth Caliph: Ali + Fatimah AD 656-661

SUNNIS   SHINAHS   KHARIJIS

Hassan   Hussain

Ali as Sajad

5th Imam: Muhammad al Baqir   Zaid

6th Imam: Jafar as Sadiq d. 765   ZAIDIS

7th Imam: Musa al Kazim d. 799   Ismail

11th Imam: Al Husan al Askari d.874   ISMAILIS (THE SEVENERS)

—— NUSAIRIS (ALAWIS)

12th Imam: Muhammad al Muntazar
(disappeared 873)

THE TWELVERS   —— DRUZES

Al Mustansir d. 1094

Nizar   Al Mustali

NIZARIS   BOHRA ISMAILIS
(MUSTALIANS)

KHOJA ISMAILIS

Mirza Hussain Ali d. 1891
The Baha Ullah (1856)

BAHAIS   ISMAILIS (FOLLOWERS OF
THE AGHA KHAN)

BIBLIOGRAPHY

Ali, Abdullah Yusuf. *The Meaning of the Holy Quran.*
New edition with revised translation and commentary,
Beltsville, Maryland, Amana Publications, 1995

Ali, Ameer. *The Spirit of Islam: a Shi'ite View of Islam.*
London, Oxford University Press, 1967

Anderson, Norman. *Islam in the Modern World: a Christian Perspective.* Leicester, Apollos, 1990

Arberry, A.J. *Sufism: an account of the Mystics of Islam.*
London, George Allen & Unwin, 1979

Beck, Lois and Keddie Nikki (editors). *Women in the Muslim World.* London, Harvard University Press, 1978

Cooper, Anne (compiler). *Ishmael my Brother: a Biblical Course on Islam.* Revised edition. Tunbridge Wells, MARC, 1993

Gilchrist, John. *Is Muhammad foretold in the Bible?*
Sheffield, FFM Publications, 1979

Gilchrist, John. *Origins and Sources of the Gospel of Barnabas.* Sheffield, FFM Publications, 1979

Goldsmith, Martin. *Islam and Christian Witness.* Revised edition. Bromley, Send the Light, 1991

Gospel of Barnabas. Translated by Lonsdale and Laura Ragg. Oxford, Clarendon Press, 1907

Hughes, Thomas Patrick. *A Dictionary of Islam.* Lahore, Kazi Publications, modern reprint of 1885 edition

Iliff, Frances P. *Salam Alekum: Understanding Muslim*

Culture to make Friends. London, Interserve, 1995

Jeffery, Patricia. *Frogs in a Well: Indian Women in Purdah.* London, Zed Press, 1979

Masood, Steven. *The Bible and The Qur'an: a Question of Integrity.* Carlisle, OM Publishing, 2001

Masood, Steven. *Into the Light: a Young Muslim's Search for Truth.* Carlisle, OM Publishing 1986

Miller, William. *The Baha'i Faith: Its History and Teaching.* Pasadena, William Carey Library, 1974

Moucarry, Chawkat Georges. *Islam and Christianity at the Crossroads.* Oxford, Lion, 1988

Musk, Bill A. *Passionate Believing: the 'Fundamentalist' Face of Islam.* Tunbridge Wells, Monarch Publications/MARC, 1992

Musk, Bill A. *The Unseen Face of Islam: Sharing the Gospel with Ordinary Muslims.* Crowborough, Monarch Publications/MARC/EMA, 1989

Nicholson, R.A. *The Mystics of Islam: Sufism.* London, Routledge & Kegan Paul, 1979

Rodinson, Maxime. *Muhammad.* 2nd English edition, translated by Anne Carter. Harmondsworth, Penguin, 1996

Stacey, Vivienne. *Women in Islam.* London, Interserve, 1995

THE ORGANISATIONS WHICH CONTRIBUTED TO THIS BOOK

FELLOWSHIP OF FAITH FOR THE MUSLIMS
P.O. Box 5864, Basildon SS13 3FF, UK
E-mail: admin@f-f-m.org.uk

The Fellowship of Faith for the Muslims (FFM) is a prayer fellowship that seeks to encourage Christians to pray for the Muslim world and so to this end publishes a regular prayer bulletin.

INSTITUTE FOR THE STUDY OF ISLAM AND CHRISTIANITY
9 & 10, Priory Row, Coventry CV1 5EX, UK

A Christian research institute focusing on the status of the Church in the Muslim world and current trends in Islam. It is also involved in training and the dissemination of information.

BARNABAS FUND
The Old Rectory, River Street, Pewsey, Wiltshire, SN9 5DB, UK
E-mail: info@barnabasfund.org

A charity supporting the suffering Church, particularly in the Muslim world, by prayer and funding for small-scale projects which help specifically Christians.